YOUR IMMUNE SYSTEM

YOUR IMMUNE SYSTEM

BY ALAN E. NOURSE, M.D.

FRANKLIN WATTS 1989
NEW YORK LONDON TORONTO SYDNEY
A VENTURE BOOK REVISED EDITION

Diagrams by: Anne Canevari Green

Photographs courtesy of:
Gamma/Liaison: p. 11 (Edmundson); Peter Arnold:
pp. 14 (Martha Cooper), 22 (Manfred Kage), 49
(Zeva Oelbaum); Photo Researchers: pp. 30 (Pasteur
Institute/Charles Dauget/Science Source), 61 (Scott
Camazine); Bettmann Archive: p. 53; American
Rheumatism Association: p. 69; Multiple Sclerosis
Society: p. 70; National Cancer Institute: p. 76.

Library of Congress Cataloging-in-Publication Data

Nourse, Alan Edward.
Your immune system / by Alan E. Nourse. — Rev. ed.
p.   cm. — (A Venture book)
Bibliography: p.
Includes index.
Summary: Discusses the workings of the body's immune defense
system; what happens when this system functions perfectly, too
vigorously, or not at all; and current research in immunology.
ISBN 0-531-10817-1
1. Immunology—Juvenile literature.   2. Immune system—Juvenile
literature.   [1. Immunology.]   I. Title.   II. Series.
QR181.8.N68   1989
616.07'9—dc20   89-8925   CIP   AC

CONTENTS

YOUR IMMUNE SYSTEM

1

YOUR IMMUNE DEFENSE SYSTEM

Would you believe that lurking beneath the quiet surface of your body you have a ferocious army of defenders busily fighting grim life-or-death battles, night and day, to protect you from alien invaders?

This is not a science-fiction story. It's the truth. That protective army is your natural *immune defense system* (usually just called the *immune system*), and the scientific study of the way it works is known as *immunology*.

Your immune system began fighting for your life soon after you were born, and—if all goes well—it will continue fighting for you through your entire life. It keeps working whether you are sick or well, happy or sad, awake or asleep. When it doesn't work properly, you can become very ill. But as long as it protects you as it should, you remain healthy in the midst of terrible dangers.

Protects you from what? From an amazing variety of things in the world around you that don't belong inside your body. Your immune system's primary task is to keep you alive, and it does that job remarkably well. If you didn't have an immune system, you might have to live in a strange, artificial world like a little boy named David.

A BODY WITHOUT DEFENSES

Not long ago David celebrated his tenth birthday, and for him that was something of a miracle. Soon after he was born, David was sealed inside a completely airtight, germ-free plastic incubator. From then on, nothing from the world outside could be allowed to come into contact with him without first being carefully treated to make it germ-free. He could not be allowed to touch another human being, not even his own parents. As he grew, he had to have larger and larger plastic "houses" in which to live. He could only go outside his germ-free cage by dressing in a plastic "space suit," like a moon-walking astronaut. On his tenth birthday his parents and friends were there to celebrate—but they all had to stay *outside* his plastic barrier.

Why couldn't David live like other people did? There was nothing wrong with the world around him, but there was something very wrong with David. While his body was developing before birth, an important part of David was left out—the immune defense system we spoke of earlier. He had no protective army inside him fighting to keep him alive—none at all.

Doctors spoke of David's rare disorder as *combined immuno deficiency disease.* All this meant was that David's body had no natural protection against the alien invaders—including the bacteria and viruses—that surround us on all sides. Nor was there any way at that

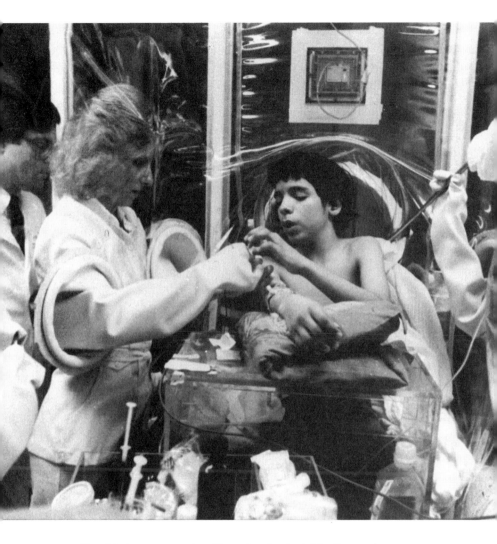

David, known as the "boy in the bubble," was born without an immune defense system, making it necessary for him to live in a sterile environment where he had no direct physical contact with other people, who might unwittingly transmit disease.

time to supply David with the immune protection his body lacked. (Today a bone-marrow transplant might have helped.) When immune protection isn't present naturally, there is usually just no substitute for it.

David's doctors knew what would happen to this boy if he were to go outside his germ-free plastic house without any immune protection and try to live like the rest of us. Very soon he would be sick with a cold, a sore throat, or an earache—and the illness would linger on and on. He would go from one infection to another in spite of antibiotics or any other treatment, until finally one infection would become so severe that medicines wouldn't be able to control it and he would die. He might survive a couple of months or years outside his germ-free house, but not much longer. But having to live in a plastic cage forever was hardly much better. After careful thought, his doctors decided to try using medicines to build up an artificial immunity in David, and then released him to live in a germ-free room in his home. Unfortunately, it didn't work. Before his twelfth birthday, David died from a series of overwhelming infections. Today doctors hope that newly discovered treatments, including bone-marrow transplants, may someday help children like David overcome their immune deficiency, but so far there is still no effective treatment.

Fortunately, David's kind of immuno deficiency disease is extremely rare. Most people are born with perfectly normal, fully active immune systems that can work for them all their lives, and up until recently doctors seldom had to deal with immune-deficiency diseases. But now, since 1980, a terrible epidemic called AIDS has been destroying the immune systems of thousands of people all over the world. AIDS is caused by a virus that invades the body and directly attacks the immune systems of formerly perfectly healthy people. With their immune systems destroyed, victims of AIDS can die just as inexorably as David did. We will say more about how this virus attacks the immune system, and the terrible damage it does, in chapter six.

THE OTHER SIDE
OF THE PICTURE

Meanwhile, many people have problems not because they lack immune defenses, but because their immune systems are working a little too vigorously.

Mary Sue K. has such a problem. On an April morning every year she wakes up sneezing violently, her eyes red, her nose itching. For the next three weeks her nose will run constantly, her ears will itch, and she will sneeze and sneeze. A special antihistamine medicine will clear up her symptoms for a few hours at a time, but they come back just as soon as the medicine wears off. Then about three weeks after they start, the symptoms go away all by themselves just as suddenly and mysteriously as they began.

Mary Sue's doctor says that she has "hay fever," caused by an allergic reaction to maple tree pollen. (No other pollens seem to bother her.) During her attacks, the moist inner lining of her nose becomes clogged with a special kind of white blood cell not normally present in such large numbers. This is a telltale sign that her immune system is fiercely *overreacting* to contact with an "alien invader"—the offending pollen—and that is exactly what an allergic reaction is. By starting a long

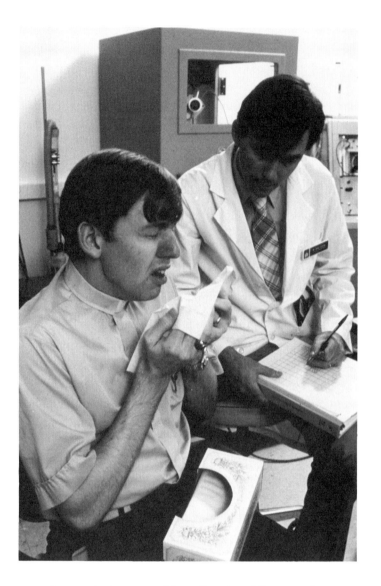

A man being tested for allergies. His sneezing and runny nose are visible signs that his immune system is responding to an allergen.

series of injections in the middle of the winter to make her body less sensitive to the pollen, Mary Sue might avoid her hay fever attack the next spring, but she prefers just to take the antihistamines for relief until the pollen goes away and the symptoms disappear on their own.

Mary Sue's hay fever is mostly just a nuisance. She is one of millions of people who have minor allergic reactions to various foreign substances they come into contact with. But Roger M., a ninth-grader, has a more serious allergic problem. Since the age of six he has had periodic attacks of *asthma*, a respiratory disease in which the tiny air tubes in the lungs squeeze shut, trapping air inside and forcing the victim to struggle and wheeze, trying to push the air out again. Roger's asthma attacks begin quite suddenly and without warning. First his chest begins to feel tight. A few moments later he is fighting for breath, coughing, and wheezing. Without the proper medicine, the attack might last all day or all night, leaving him exhausted. To prevent this, he must take pills every day and use a small medicinal inhaler to help keep his air tubules relaxed. This helps prevent attacks.

Asthma is not always caused by allergies alone; it can arise from many different sources. But allergies often play an important part. In Roger's case, his asthma results, in part, from an allergic reaction to the mold spores that are found in ordinary house dust. To help him avoid contact with these "alien invaders," Roger's bedroom is now fitted with special air filters, and everyone in his family works hard to keep dust from accumulating. His asthma attacks are never life-threatening, and they always go away sooner or later, but they are a thoroughly frightening and unpleasant health problem just the same. Unfortunately, Roger may have asthma for the rest of his life. His natural immune system is working so hard protecting him from a foreign substance—mold spores—that it actually makes him far sicker than the mold spores alone could possibly make him.

At age thirteen Kathy D. had an even more frightening allergic problem. Kathy didn't think she was allergic to anything until one day at summer camp when she was stung by a bee—and thought she was going to die as a result of it. Right away her eyelids grew puffy, and huge, itchy bumps appeared all over her body. A few moments later her voice went hoarse, breathing became difficult, and she almost became unconscious. Fortunately, the camp nurse recognized what was happening and injected her with a medicine called Adrenalin to quiet the attack long enough to get her to a nearby hospital emergency room. There, other treatment restored Kathy's abnormally low blood pressure and soon put an end to her sudden and frightening attack. The doctor said she had suffered an *anaphylactic shock*—a sudden, massive overreaction of her body's immune system to an alien invader, in this case the venom from a bee sting. On rare occasions, people may have similar violent reactions to penicillin, horse serum, or other medicines. Fortunately, such severe reactions to bee stings aren't very common—most people have only a little harmless burning and swelling after a sting. But when it does occur, such a reaction can be very dangerous unless the proper medicine is available and quickly administered. Kathy now carries a "bee-sting kit" of emergency medicines wherever she goes. In addition, she is undergoing treatment to make her body less sensitive to bee venom so the next bee sting will not affect her so seriously.

A TWO-EDGED SWORD

In the last three cases, the body's immune system has been overdoing its job of protecting these young people against the invasion of relatively trivial foreign substances. Usually allergies are just a minor nuisance, but in some people they become serious health problems, and on occasion they might even threaten life. But in each case the same basic sequence of events has occurred. First, some foreign substance has found entry into the body. Next, in sharp response, the immune system has sprung into action against the invader and—in these cases—has done its job too well.

Obviously your immune system is a powerful weapon, absolutely necessary to keep you alive—yet it can be a two-edged sword. When it isn't working properly, people like David and thousands of AIDS victims get sick and die. When it does its job too well, people can also get sick.

But for most people, the immune system does far more good than harm. It is a very important and very complex part of the way your healthy body works to stay healthy. It has a real and vital purpose. And although many people experience annoying allergic reactions of one sort or another sometimes in their lives, the immune system mostly does its protective work quietly and unobtrusively—and we survive because of it.

But what, exactly, *is* the body's immune defense system? What is its job, and how does it go about doing it? What are the "alien invaders" it protects us from? To find answers to these questions, we must first see what scientists have learned, bit by bit over the years, about this complex and amazing internal defense system.

2

ANTIGENS AND ANTIBODIES

Ever since the microscope was invented over 250 years ago, scientists have realized that we live in a world teeming with tiny living organisms far too small to be seen with the naked eye. They are in the air we breathe, the ground we walk on, the water of our lakes and ponds. They are found on every object we touch, in the clothes we wear, and all over the surface of our bodies. These so-called microorganisms include *bacteria* (one-celled plantlike organisms); tiny animal-like organisms called *protozoa*; *fungi* (another form of simple plant life); and multitudes of different *viruses*.

Fortunately for us, most of these microorganisms are quite harmless. Many actually do useful things, such as decaying dead vegetation, helping us to digest and absorb our food, or getting rid of waste materials. But when some gain a foothold inside of us, they can grow and multiply to cause dangerous infectious diseases. A few, such as the influenza viruses, or the salmonella bacteria that cause food poisoning, merely make us temporarily ill. But others—such as the polio viruses, the tetanus (lockjaw) bacteria, or the streptococcus organisms—can easily cripple or even kill us if they just get the chance. If our bodies did not have a built-in protection against these potential killers, the world would be a very dangerous place to live in, and we would not last long in it.

Of course, the skin covering our bodies helps to keep these organisms out. But the warm, moist membranes inside our noses and throats, our intestinal tracts, and our lungs, for instance, provide these invaders with easy entry. They can also enter the body through cuts and abrasions in the skin. And once inside, they can travel in the bloodstream to cause destructive infections in the brain, lungs, spinal cord, kidneys, urinary bladder, intestine, or any other organ. Viruses actually invade our bodies' cells themselves and can ultimately destroy nerve, brain, or lung tissue. The human body has just the right temperature to allow these organisms to grow rapidly and provides all kinds of nutrients on which they can feed.

In short, without some kind of internal protection, we would be coming down with dangerous infections almost constantly. That we ordinarily have only occasional infections, and then usually get over them, tells us that we *do* have a natural protective system that keeps these invaders from overwhelming us. We call that internal protective system the *immune system*.

THE NICE PHAGOCYTES

Most of what we know about our immune system has been learned only in the last twenty-five years or so. But a few parts of the picture were pieced together almost a hundred years ago. As early as 1888, for example, a Russian biologist named Élie Metchnikoff, working in

Paris, discovered that blood contains not only the red blood cells that were seen under the earliest microscopes but also a number of much larger, colorless cells—the white blood cells. These amoebalike white cells seemed to roam about the body at random, scooping up bits of cellular debris and other cast-off materials like tiny garbage collectors. They also seemed to scoop up infectious bacteria they encountered in their wanderings—and to eat them! Metchnikoff called these white cells *phagocytes*, from Greek words meaning "cells that eat." It soon became clear that whenever a bacterial infection started somewhere in the body, these "nice phagocytes," as Metchnikoff described them, would quickly gather in the area in great numbers and begin battling the bacteria, destroying many of the invaders on the spot—and being destroyed themselves in turn. In fact, the pus that often formed in an infected area was found to be made up largely of dead white blood cells along with millions of dead bacteria. One type of white cell was much larger than the others and did an even better job of killing bacteria. Metchnikoff called these cells *macrophages*, or "big eaters."

About the same time that Metchnikoff was studying his "nice phagocytes" another biologist named Emil von Behring was discovering that people who had survived an attack of diphtheria had a kind of chemical substance in their blood serum (the fluid part of the blood) that was capable of neutralizing a vicious poison, or *toxin*, given off by the diphtheria bacilli. People who had never been infected with diphtheria had none of this *antitoxin* in their blood. On the heels of this discovery, in the 1890s, other scientists found that many people had other substances in the blood—not phagocytes, but dissolved chemical substances that seemed capable of destroying

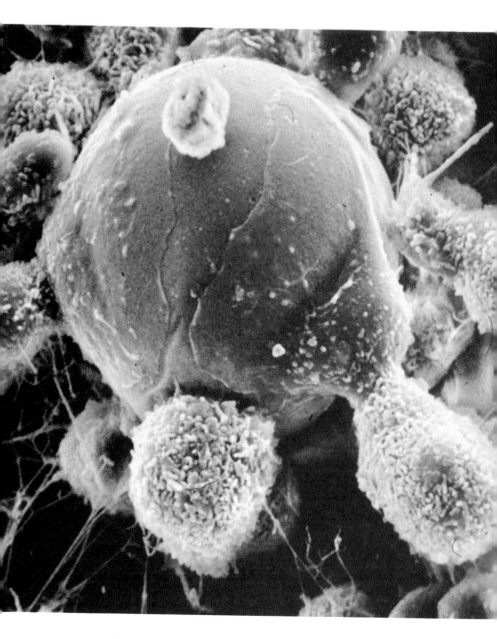

A macrophage destroying a foreign substance

bacteria. Thus, as early as 1900 it was recognized that the human body actually possessed two different kinds of built-in protection against invading microorganisms: a *cellular defense system*, made up of Metchnikoff's phagocytes and macrophages; and a *serum defense system* (now called the *humoral defense system*), which included both antitoxins that neutralized bacterial poisons and other chemical substances floating in the bloodstream that seemed to destroy bacteria.

THE ANTIBODY ARMY

What exactly were those "other chemical substances" in the bloodstream? For many years nobody knew for sure. Then in the 1930s, laboratory scientists discovered a way to separate out individual kinds of proteins from among the many different kinds that form the major building blocks of our organs and tissues. Since then, researchers have learned a great deal about these "other substances" and how they behave when faced by alien invaders such as bacteria or viruses.

First of all, these substances proved to be exactly the same kind of chemicals as the antitoxin against diphtheria, except that they seemed to affect bacteria or viruses instead of toxins. They were all special protein molecules that would appear in the bloodstream in enormous numbers shortly after bacteria, bacterial poisons, or viruses had invaded the body. The exact physical shape that these protein molecules took was found to be extremely interesting. In each different invasion they seemed to be carefully form-fitted or shaped to match certain *surface-marker molecules* found on the surface of the invading microorganisms or poisons. In each case, these special serum proteins would fit only one type of surface-marker molecule, like keys built especially to fit one—and only one—lock. Because they seemed to be made to order—to fit perfectly and attach themselves to the surface-marker molecules on specific invading organisms or poisons—they all came to be called *antibodies*. Once attached to the outside surface of invading organisms, the antibodies seemed to make it easier for the phagocytes to eat them. Because the individual surface-marker molecules on these organisms seemed to be the things that stimulated or triggered the manufacture of specially shaped antibodies, they came to be known as "anti(body)-generators," or simply *antigens*. (See figure 1.)

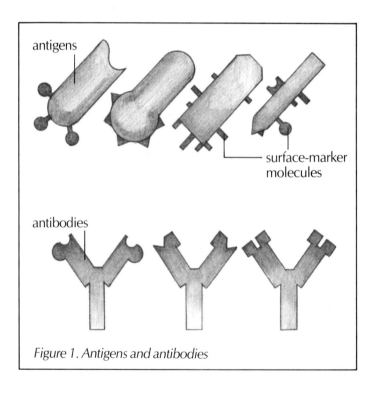

Figure 1. Antigens and antibodies

IMMUNOGLOBULINS
ON THE MARCH

All these antibody proteins seem to have certain things in common. All of them, for example, belong to a class of proteins known as *gamma globulins*. Because these proteins seemed to be involved in our immune defense system, scientists called them *immunoglobulins* or "Ig's" for short. Soon it was found that there were several different families of Ig's. One family, known as immunoglobulin A, or IgA, was made up of rather large, clumsy protein molecules that always seemed to appear in the body's fluid secretions—in saliva, for instance, or tears, or in the mucus secreted in the air tubules, or in secretions from the stomach or intestine. These seemed to be sensible places for antibodies to turn up to fight invading organisms, since bacteria and viruses often found entry into the body through moist mucous membranes. IgA was also found in a mother's breast milk after the birth of a baby—an important point we will come back to soon.

Two other families of Ig antibodies might be thought of as the "little guys" and the "big guys." The "little guys" were quite small Ig protein molecules and were called immunoglobulin G (IgG). The "big guys" were larger, more complex protein molecules called immunoglobulin M (IgM). Both IgG and IgM were found, not in secretions of the body, but rather floating in the bloodstream itself. Both would make their way directly to the area where the alien invader was breaking in and then clamp themselves onto the surface-marker molecules they were manufactured to fit.

At first they seemed much the same, except that IgM antibodies were a little bigger and appeared in the blood a little faster than IgG molecules. But now scientists know there are some very important differences. Although IgM antibodies appear in the bloodstream much more rapidly than IgG antibodies when a foreign invader attacks—within as little as twenty-four hours—they only last a few days to a few weeks. The IgG antibodies take several days to appear, but then they may remain in the bloodstream for weeks or even years longer.

What is more, the difference in size of these two Ig's is significant. When a new baby is born, it has no antibodies of its own to protect it because it has never been exposed to alien invaders such as bacteria or viruses and thus nothing has triggered the manufacture of antibodies. Besides, the baby's rudimentary immune system is very immature and unable to mount an effective immune defense. This means that for the first few months of life the baby would be an easy victim for any infection that came along, except for one thing—the Ig antibodies it has received from its mother while it is still developing. The baby's mother has in her bloodstream antibodies against all kinds of infections she has had in the past. Because the IgG antibody molecules are so small, they can make their way through the placenta into the fetus's bloodstream from the mother before the baby is born. IgM molecules are just too big to get through from mother to baby. But the IgG antibodies, together with the IgA antibodies from the mother's milk (if the baby is nursed), are enough to provide early protection. As the baby's first weeks and months of life pass, these antibodies from the mother gradually break down and disappear. But by then the newborn baby's own immune system has matured. It has been exposed to enough infection that its own antibody factories are ready for work and it doesn't need special protection anymore.

Finally, there is another form of immunoglobulin known as IgE. IgE also circulates in the bloodstream, like IgG and IgM, but because of individual heredity, some people's bodies produce vastly greater amounts of IgE than others do in the face of some alien invaders. There is evidence that these are the people who tend to have troublesome allergic reactions—which we'll talk about more in chapter five.

Thus every normal person's body, from the age of a few months on, has a built-in ability to manufacture a veritable army of his or her own Ig antibodies on command whenever a foreign invader comes along—an antibody army perfectly matched to each specific alien-invader antigen or surface marker and ready to fight off each new infection. *But what gives the command?* Where do these antibody armies come from? How does the body know exactly what shape antibody is needed in the first place? Once the antibodies are formed, *how* do they attach themselves so perfectly to the surface of these invaders before they can do harm? Each of these questions involves a fascinating story.

3

THE MYSTERIOUS LYMPHOCYTES

Antibodies do not just happen to be around in the right form whenever we happen to need them. As we have seen, a child has none of its own when it is born—only a few passed on from its mother. The baby's own antibodies appear in the bloodstream only after an alien invader has gained a foothold somewhere in the body. Only then are the baby's antibodies literally manufactured to order with precisely the right physical shape to clamp onto special surface markers carried by the invaders. Clearly there must be some kind of "antibody factory" somewhere in the body capable of hammering out exactly the right-shaped antibodies in large quantities when the need arises.

In 1948 immunologists finally identified that "antibody factory." Antibodies, they found, were manufactured by special cells called *plasma cells* scattered throughout the bone marrow and in glandlike structures known as *lymph nodes* located all over the body. In fact, the plasma cells themselves seemed to be formed as needed out of other cells known as *lymphocytes*, specifically for the job of antibody-making.

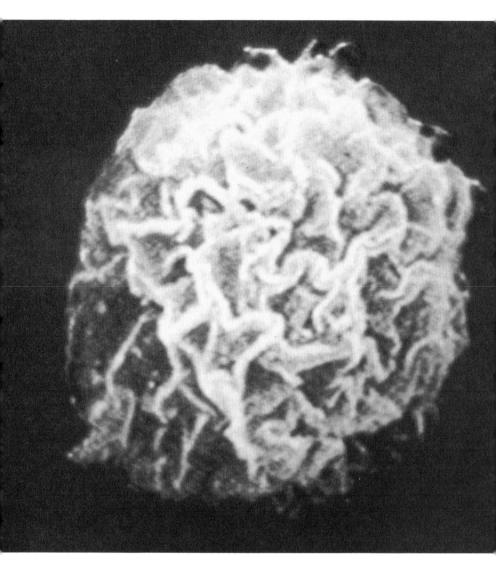

This lymphocyte is a member of one class of white blood cells that play many important roles in the body's immune defense system.

To the immunologists, this was a very important discovery. Scientists had known for years that lymphocytes existed in the body, but they really had no idea what they were there for. Lymphocytes seemed to be formed either in the bone marrow or in the lymph nodes—little glandular lumps of tissue scattered hither and yon throughout the body. Whole clusters of lymph nodes are located in the throat, for example, just beneath the tonsils, and often become swollen and tender when we develop tonsillitis or strep throat. Other clusters are found in the armpits, the groin, behind the knees, or around many of the joints. These, too, become tender and enlarged whenever an infection occurs nearby. Other lymph nodes are tucked in around the base of the lungs or the great blood vessels deep in the chest, or scattered throughout the abdomen. And the lymphocytes manufactured in these lymph nodes have long been known to find their way into the blood as another kind of white blood cell, similar to Metchnikoff's phagocytes except that lymphocytes are much smaller. Unlike the phagocytes, they seem to be made up mostly of nucleus and don't seem to devour bacteria the way phagocytes do. Ordinarily about 25 to 30 percent of the white cells in the blood are lymphocytes, but during certain kinds of viral infections, for instance, many more appear in the bloodstream.

Lymphocytes have another odd quality: they are among the longest-lived cells in the body. Red blood cells only live about three weeks before they disintegrate, to be replaced by new ones. Other cells in the body are constantly being lost and replaced, owing to wear and tear. In contrast, lymphocytes were found to live as long as six or seven years!

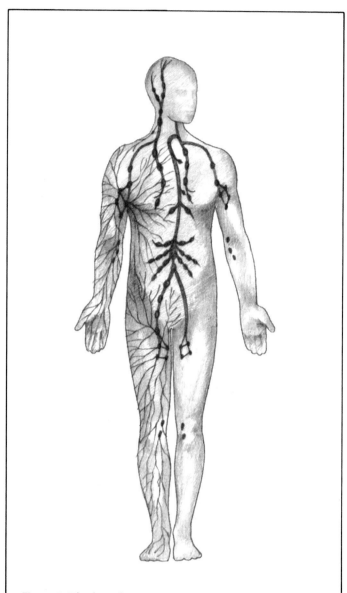

Figure 2. The lymphatic system

But what did these long-lived lymphocytes *do?* They didn't seem to chase and devour bacteria the way phagocytes did. In fact, they seemed to spend most of their time just drifting about in the bloodstream or traveling from one lymph node to another by way of special *lymph channels* that carry body fluids through the bays and backwaters that exist between the body's cells. It was not until the late 1940s and early 1950s that immunologists made the startling discovery that the lymphocytes were really the very foundation stones of the body's immune protective system.

B-CELLS AND T-CELLS

In recent years, scientists have learned a great deal about these mysterious lymphocytes. For one thing, they are not all the same, although many of them look identical under a microscope. There are several different kinds, and each kind has a different job to do to keep the immune system running.

One group of lymphocytes are formed in the bone marrow from primitive cells called *stem cells* or "cell-makers." Because of their bone marrow origin, these cells are called B-lymphocytes or *B-cells* for short. While they are still young, the B-cells migrate to the lymph nodes, where they stand ready to mature into antibody-making *plasma cells* when they get the signal that an alien invader has found entry.

A second group of lymphocytes are the signal-carriers. These cells, while they are still young, mature or "grow up" in the *thymus gland*, a small gland that lies in the upper part of the chest. There, scientists believe, these lymphocytes are somehow *activated* by thymus gland hormones or other chemicals which direct their future jobs. And because of this lasting thymus gland influence, these cells are called T-lymphocytes, or *T-cells* for short.

From the first the T-cells seem far busier and more vigorous than the B-cells. One group, as we will see, must bring word of the alien invader to the B-cells, telling them which antibodies are desperately needed. Another group of T-cells, called *T-helper cells*, spur on the swift manufacture of antibodies to fight the invader. Yet another group, called *T-suppressor cells*, help shut down the antibody factories when the threat of the invasion is passed.

The lymphocytes as a group have another very special built-in quality that seems almost incredible at first glance—a pre-existing ability to be *activated* or "alerted" to virtually any kind of foreign-invader antigen in existence before that foreign invader comes anywhere near the body. Of course the lymphocytes, like all body cells, contain the genetic materials that make *their* human body absolutely unique—the "self" quality that makes each person in the world uniquely different from any other person. (Even identical twins who have developed from a single fertilized egg with exactly the same genetic materials become slightly different with time.) But lymphocytes are also genetically prepared, *in advance*, to be alerted by any foreign invader that might come along.

Let's see in a little more detail how all these mysterious lymphocytes work together with each other and with other parts of the immune system—the phagocytes and macrophages, for instance—to protect us against alien invaders.

SOLDIERS ON PATROL

Although lymphocytes do not seem to attack bacteria directly, many of the T-cells do wander constantly through all parts of the body. Scientists have actually tagged these tiny cells with radioactive markers and then followed them in their travels. And what they do along the way is remarkable indeed.

Carried to all parts of the body by the bloodstream, these small, pale cells wiggle and twist right through the walls of tiny blood vessels and come into contact with tissue cells in all parts of the body. They thread their way through the spaces between the cells in all of our organs, constantly meeting up with cells and body fluids everywhere, acting for all the world like soldiers on patrol in their own territory in search of enemy infiltrators. Everywhere they go they touch the special surface markers that identify every cell they contact. We can almost imagine them calling out, "Who goes there?" and then waiting for the password that indicates that the cell or protein they have just encountered is really "one of our boys," possessing the natural "self" quality that marks everything that belongs inside each person's own body and nobody else's. When the right password comes back—we might call it the "self" password—the lymphocyte drifts onto another cell, and then another and another, constantly challenging everywhere it goes.

Presently the lymphocyte drifts into a wider fluid-filled space between the cells—the beginnings of a lymph channel. Here it is washed along into larger and larger lymph channels and finally back to a lymph node again, much the way a patrolling soldier would eventually return to headquarters to report that all was well.

Then the lymphocyte goes out into the bloodstream again and travels to another part of the body to begin a similar cycle of exploration, challenging and testing and identifying the cells that it touches as "self" and therefore "all right."

In each human body there are literally billions of such lymphocytes constantly infiltrating the tissues, constantly returning to the lymph nodes to "report," and then repeating the cycle over and over. And thanks in part to their long lives, we might say they survive long enough to "know the country" thoroughly as they patrol the body ceaselessly, night and day.

"SELF" AND "NOT-SELF"

Now suppose that a deadly bacterial cell finds its way inside a person's body—a poison-producing streptococcus, for example, capable of causing a dangerous disease such as scarlet fever. It begins growing and multiplying in the soft, moist mucous membrane at the back of the throat, forming more and more streptococci and pouring out a toxin that damages the body's healthy tissue cells and dissolves red blood cells.

Within a very short time, perhaps even within a few minutes, several things begin to happen in rapid succession. First, macrophages that happen to be in the vicinity of the new invasion are drawn to the site and immediately begin engulfing and digesting the invading bacteria. Even while these macrophages are at work, large numbers of patrolling T-cells in the area appear, some of them with preformed antigen receptors already built in, ready to be activated by contact with a foreign antigen. These T-cells, in cooperation with the macrophages, recognize that a foreign invader is present.

Essentially these immune system cells, working together, identify the invading streptococcus, challenge it, and demand the password.

But this time the password that comes back is wrong. The surface markers or antigen carried by the streptococcus, unlike the "self" markers on cells that naturally belong in the body, are "not-self" markers identifying a dangerous foreign invader, capable of killing us if it is not stopped.

When the T-cells recognize this, their pattern of behavior changes dramatically. Most of them remain at the invasion site and direct a *local inflammatory reaction*—tiny blood vessels swell, fluid pours out into the tissue, and the victim begins developing a fever. At the same time, great numbers of the nice phagocytes are "called" to the area to fight the invading bacteria by a kind of chemical alarm system called *chemotaxis*. At the battle site, the phagocytes try their best to destroy the streptococci. Sometimes they win, and sometimes they themselves are killed. The poisons poured out by the streptococcal germs may destroy hundreds of thousands or millions of these white cells, so that the battlefield is soon littered with dead white cells, dead bacteria, and fragments of dead cell bodies. But win or lose, the phagocytes may at least slow the spread of the infection until another, different wave of warriors arrive.

These next warriors are the antibodies we spoke of earlier.

At the time of first contact with the "not-self" markers of the invading bacteria, the T-cells with preformed antigen receptors built in make their way into the nearest lymph channel and high-tail it for the closest home lymph node. These T-cells have done more than merely recognize a "not-self" enemy in the body. Their antigen receptors have been activated by exposure to the foreign antigen, so they carry back a pattern of the invader's "not-self" surface markers, much as a tailor might carry a pattern back to his shop after accurately measuring a person for a suit. On arriving at lymph node headquarters, these antigen-activated T-cells find B-cells that also carry the right preformed antigen receptors, and activate them.

These activated B-cells then undergo some remarkable transformations. First, each activated cell begins *proliferating*—reproducing itself—until each one of thousands of activated cells have formed whole clusters of exact duplicates, each cell carrying the antigen pattern. Then the B-cells begin maturing and changing. Some simply change into *memory cells* which carry and hold an accurate molecular memory of the shape of the alien antigen—permanently—so the body won't ever forget it. Other B-cells, prodded on by T-helper cells, undergo an even more profound transformation. Fully activated and stimulated by the foreign antigen, they reproduce and mature into totally different cells— *plasma cells* or "antibody factories." And then, without delay, these plasma cells begin manufacturing antibody proteins to fit that specific antigen as fast as they can, pouring them out into the bloodstream as rapidly as they are made.

Of course these events take time. It may be days or even longer before large numbers of form-fitted antibody molecules turn up in the bloodstream or reach the site of the streptococci invasion. To understand what happens when they do arrive, we need to know something about still another weapon in the immune system armory.

THE REMARKABLE ROLE
OF COMPLEMENT

When antibodies appear at the site of infection, they attach themselves to the surface markers of the invading organisms, causing them to clump together and making it easier for the phagocytes to engulf and destroy them. But the antibodies have another job to do as well. Once attached to the invader's surface, they are ready to trigger a remarkable chain reaction.

Antibodies are really nothing more than a group of very special protein molecules. At some point in the evolution of human beings into the form they have today, another group of special protein molecules also came to be present in the bloodstream. These proteins are *not* antibodies; they are *not* formed by plasma cells, and they are *not* made directly in response to the presence of any foreign antigen. Rather, they are present in the bloodstream all the time, just waiting for the right sequence of events to happen.

Scientists have found at least nine different forms of molecule in this particular family of proteins. These nine forms, taken together, have been given the rather odd name of *complement* because when they were first discovered it was mistakenly assumed that their job was to "complement" (that is, to help or assist) antibodies in destroying invading bacteria. We now know that this was exactly backward. It is the antibodies that help or assist the complement molecules to fit together and transform themselves into a powerful bacteria-killer, and then point out which cell the complement should kill.

Imagine for a moment that a powerful rifle is lying on the table in nine separate pieces. Any of the pieces alone is perfectly harmless. Even all nine pieces are harmless when they are lying separate on the table. It is only when all those pieces have been assembled in exactly the right way, and in exactly the right order, that the rifle becomes a dangerous weapon. When that has happened, the rifle is not very safe to have around—it might go off accidentally, or be fired in the wrong direction instead of at the proper target.

The nine complement proteins work much like the pieces of the rifle. Once an antibody protein has clamped itself onto the surface marker of an invading cell, it provides a hooking-on place for the first of the nine different complement molecules floating around in the blood. That complement molecule provides a hooking-on place for the second complement protein, which in turn provides a place for the third to hook onto, and so forth. Only when all nine forms are hooked together in the right order does this long chain of complement molecules become armed, like an assembled rifle, capable of exploding and punching a hole in the wall of the nearest cell.

However, the complement complex is blind. It doesn't care *which* cell it attacks. The nearest cell around will do. This, of course, could be very dangerous to normal body cells except for one thing: the complement complex isn't strung together at all until the first molecule becomes attached to an antibody molecule clamped to the surface marker of a specific target cell. Under these circumstances, of course, with the armed complement attached to its surface, the invading enemy cell *is* the nearest cell around. The complement attached to it then becomes a cell-killer and punches a hole through the enemy cell wall, allowing fluid outside to flow in, so that the enemy cell swells up and bursts.

This, then, is one of the major jobs that antibodies do. They assemble the "complement rifle," point it at a specific target cell, and then pull the trigger. The invading cell is killed by the complement, while the body's own cells are protected from harm—and this peculiar battle can help put an end to infection. Faced with a swarm of specific antibody molecules working in cooperation with an efficient, deadly cell-killer like the "complement rifle," the bacteria are destroyed and the infection heals.

A SECOND INVASION

What we have been describing is a rough outline of how your body's immune system reacts the first time a dangerous foreigner like a streptococcus germ invades the body and sets up housekeeping. That first invasion may actually cause a severe infection before it is repelled, because of the time it takes the immune system to react. It takes time for the B-cells to reproduce themselves in large numbers after receiving the T-cells' "foreign invader" message, and still more time for the plasma cell antibody factories to make the right antibodies. For a while after the battle is won, those antibodies that are not used up conquering the infection continue to circulate in the bloodstream. More and more antibodies might still be manufactured, too, except for the T-suppressor cells that now block or slow down antibody production in the plasma cells. What actually happens is that gradually, over weeks or months, those antibodies slowly disappear from the bloodstream.

So what happens, then, if that same dangerous foreigner tries to invade the body a second time, long after the first invasion has been beaten off? What happens is that a second antibody reaction immediately occurs, much faster and more vigorous than the first—because the immune system *remembers the invader* and is ready to pounce almost instantly any time that same foreign antigen appears again. You'll remember that some of the B-cells in the lymph nodes originally changed into *memory cells* carrying the exact lock-and-key shape of antibodies against the alien surface markers—for instant future reference, so to speak. The T-cells and plasma cells carrying the alien markers also remain primed, ready to resume producing precisely the right antibodies at the drop of a hat anytime that same alien invader should reappear, with far less "lag time" than before. Thus, any invader with those same "not-self" markers will be hit much faster and harder than the first time— so swiftly, in fact, that an active infection has no chance to get started at all. In some cases the only way to tell for sure that an invader has made a second attempt at infection is to discover, by lab tests, a sudden and otherwise unexplained rise in the level, or "titer," of antibodies against that particular antigen in the bloodstream. We will come back to this point in chapter four, when we see how the process of vaccination or immunization makes it possible to build up antibody levels against certain dangerous invaders *in advance*, so that no active infection by those invaders ever has a chance to take place.

ENTER THE "KILLER CELLS"

By means of the marvelous and intricate mechanism we have discussed above, specific antibodies are formed very quickly against alien-invader antigens that find their way into the body. The antibody molecules latch onto surface markers on the alien cells. There they not only inactivate or clump the invading bacteria together, but also "fix" or trigger the complement protein complex, which becomes an efficient cell-killer to help rid the body of the dangerous invaders. Everything depends on the antibodies that are formed when B-cells, activated by the invader's antigens, transform themselves into plasma cells and become veritable antibody factories. As we have seen, the complex partnership action of macrophages, T-cells, B-cells, memory cells, plasma cells, and antibodies and complement—all working together—form a highly efficient defense system to stop what could otherwise lead to dangerous infection or even death—as long as the whole immune system is in perfect working order.

Sometimes, however, the body faces a different, more subtle kind of invader that presents such an extraordinary threat that the immune system needs still another type of lymphocyte to deal with it. Unlike T-cells or B-cells, these large, grainy-looking lymphocytes, also influenced by the thymus gland, can become transformed into something far more grim than any ordinary lymphocyte under the right circumstances. In fact, they can change into such fiercely aggressive traveling cell-destroyers that immunologists have dubbed them "natural killer cells," or *NK cells*.

These potentially murderous NK cells are, in a sense, the advance hatchet men of the immune system. As it happens, certain alien invaders are very clever about the way they invade the body. Some viruses, for example, can work their way inside our body's own cells and hide there. They may leave telltale "footprints" outside the cells in the form of foreign proteins—antigens—that indicate that they have been around, but the infectious part of the virus—its core of nucleic acid—is buried inside apparently normal cells, either forcing them to manufacture more virus particles or, in some cases, just hiding out indefinitely. Thus, in a subtle way, those normal cells have been turned into "not-self" cells masquerading as "self" cells. In other cases, normal body cells may undergo certain dangerous internal changes and become transformed into cancer cells. When this happens, the usual "self" markers on those cells may alter very slightly. They still *seem* to be "self" cells, but there is something about them that the immune system senses isn't right. In some odd way they also seem to be "not-self."

When something like this happens, the antibody-complement defense system that does such a good job of stopping a bacterial invasion may just not be up to the task that it faces. Patrolling T-cells may only sense "self" and not recognize any "not-self" antigens because they are hidden inside apparently normal body cells. Antibodies may be made, but may not be fully effective, so that the virus-invaded cells or the cancer-altered cells are not destroyed. But the NK cells recognize *something* is wrong, and pour out of the bloodstream into the invasion area. Here these killer lymphocytes surround the virus-invaded cells or the newly transformed cancer cells and launch a virulent, all-out attack—and the more "not-self" the invader appears, the more effective the attack.

Such killer-cell attacks have actually been photographed and these battles very much resemble hand-to-hand combat. The killer lymphocytes surround the altered cell on all sides. Then they appear to start beating on it, prodding and poking and pushing it, but in fact they are pouring out cell-poisoning chemicals. Presently the altered cell's nucleus begins to change and break apart, and the cell itself finally disintegrates.

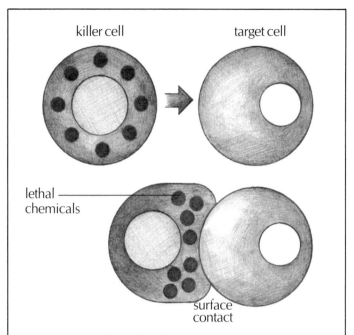

killer cell   target cell

lethal
chemicals

surface
contact

Figure 3. The killer cell makes contact with the target
cell, orients its weapons toward the target, and delivers a
burst of lethal chemicals.

In certain ways, the behavior of these killer cells, busily destroying cells that seem like normal body cells but really aren't, comes dangerously close to something more than just a protective system. If the killer cells were to leave some of the altered cells unharmed, the alien invader might press on and ultimately win the battle. But if the killer cells should happen to make a mistake about their targets, they could do enormous damage to perfectly normal, innocent body cells. Immunologists today believe that this actually happens sometimes and may be the underlying cause of some familiar human diseases. (See chapter five.) But under normal circumstances these dangerous killer cells are constantly monitored or checked—and controlled—by T-cells. Much is yet to be learned about how this control system works. But when it works as it should, the end result is a marvelously delicate balancing act, in which the killer cells are used like precision scalpel blades, cutting out and destroying dangerous cells while leaving truly normal cells untouched. With their activity, the immune system becomes a carefully regulated weapon to protect us from damage and preserve our lives.

4

THE IMMUNE SYSTEM AS HERO

Obviously, our bodies do not rely on a single simple immune system that always works the same way whenever the body is threatened by foreign invaders. The system actually is made up of several different and highly complex systems, each designed to protect the body in a different way. When an invasion takes place, all of the systems work together, but the particular part that will predominate in any given case will depend on the nature of the invader as determined by the ceaselessly wandering T-cells.

Each year immunologists discover more about the busy activity of this multiple protective system. Although much still remains to be learned, it is clear that the proper functioning of the immune system depends heavily on a series of fail-safe mechanisms and delicate controls that regulate all of its parts. The immune system is both very powerful and, potentially, very dangerous. As long as it works exactly as it should, it is truly the hero of the body, providing us with vital life-sustaining protection against a hostile outside world. But anytime it veers off target even slightly, it can become very harmful.

THE PERFECTLY
FUNCTIONING SYSTEM

What does the immune system actually accomplish for us when it is working as it should? The work it does seems more and more remarkable the more scientists learn about it.

First, as we have seen, it provides us with an aggressive first line of defense against invasions by dangerous microorganisms of all kinds. It enables us to throw off viral infections such as colds, influenza, rubeola, or mumps within a matter of a few days, usually with no serious complications or side effects. It strikes down bacterial infections caused by streptococci, pneumococci, or pertussis (whooping cough) organisms. It carries on a lifelong, running battle against the many strains of staphylococcus organisms that live on the body's surface and can cause lingering infections of the skin and underlying tissues whenever they get beneath the surface. Before we had protective vaccines, those who survived dangerous infections such as diphtheria, typhoid fever, smallpox, tetanus, or poliomyelitis did so because of the first line of defense provided by the immune system. Indeed, the immune system not only attacked the infecting organisms themselves but also provided protective antitoxins to neutralize the deadly poisons that otherwise could do terrible damage to brain or nerve cells, kidney tissue, or heart muscle.

Perhaps even more important, the immune system also provides a *second* line of defense against these major infections. Because some antibodies left over after a first infection remain in the bloodstream for prolonged periods, and because T-cells and memory B-cells carry molecular memories of the surface markers of an earlier

This girl is being inoculated with measles vaccine, a weakened form of the actual measles virus.

invader, the immune system remains primed to produce more antibodies very swiftly whenever necessary in the future. This means that a person who has once recovered from a dangerous infectious disease has continuing stand-by protection against reinfection for long periods, often for life. A person who has recovered from red measles (rubeola) will never have another attack because the virus that causes the disease will be stopped the moment it reappears. A person who recovers from scarlet fever will never have scarlet fever again, even though he or she may have later infections caused by other strains of streptococci. The immune system provides long-term protection against re-exposure. Add on the transfer of a mother's protective antibodies to her baby to guard it during the early months of life, and the immune system provides protection from cradle to grave.

This protection is not confined just to protecting us against living microorganisms. We are constantly exposed to a wide variety of other foreign proteins as well, some of which are absorbed into the body. These, too, can act as foreign antigens and trigger immune reactions just as well as the protein surface markers on bacteria or viruses do. Plant pollens, animal hair or dander, protein material from foods, bee or ant venoms, or irritating chemicals such as the oils from poison ivy leaves—indeed, virtually any foreign protein material with which we come into contact—can stimulate the immune system to go into action.

In many cases we aren't quite sure *why* the immune system girds up to do battle with some of these substances, since they seem to be comparatively harmless. Many of them are practically unavoidable; some are even important parts of the foods we eat. And in a sense, the immune system makes practical exceptions. For example, in the intestine, the immune system learns to "tolerate" foreign protein passing through the intestine. That is how we can all eat! Yet at the same time, the immune system in the intestine is programmed to repel the foreign antigens of typhoid fever or salmonella bacteria *invading* the intestinal wall.

Some *people* are exceptional, too. It might not seem to make sense that the immune system makes no distinction between a foreign protein antigen on the surface of a deadly infectious microorganism, on the one hand, and the essentially harmless antigen on the surface of a pollen grain, a molecule of wheat protein, or even a protein from cow's milk. But the immune system may not be entirely to blame. True, all it can do is distinguish between "self" markers and "not-self" markers—and any "not-self" marker, however, harmless it may actually be, is enough to send off the alarm. But immunologists now believe that people who have troublesome allergic problems with basically harmless antigens are genetically different from others—programmed by their heredity to respond to these antigens with hordes of IgE antibodies that lead to their allergic symptoms—while most people's immune systems tolerate these antigens and don't produce symptoms at all. Immunologists think that at one time in our evolution these high levels of IgE antibodies were a life-saving defense against parasites— but now they are more a nuisance than a protection.

VACCINATION AND IMMUNIZATION

Long before anyone even knew that there was such a thing as an immune system, physicians were putting it to work protecting people *in advance* from certain serious infections, so that they were safe from, or *immune to*, trouble when the invading organism finally did get into the body. This involves the procedure we commonly speak of as *vaccination*, or *immunization*.

In 1796 an English physician named Edward Jenner inoculated a farm boy with serum from a cowpox sore on a dairymaid's hand, and proved that thereafter the boy could not contract the far more dangerous smallpox disease that was so widespread at the time. This was the world's first deliberate vaccination—but Jenner had no idea *why* this procedure prevented smallpox. In his day, nobody had ever heard of a virus. All he knew was that people who had had the mild cowpox infection never seemed to get smallpox, even when people on all sides of them were becoming infected and dying of it.

Some ninety years later Louis Pasteur made the courageous—and very risky—decision to inoculate a boy who had been bitten by a rabid dog with some specially treated infectious material from some rabbits that had died from rabies. Pasteur didn't know what a virus was, either. All he had observed was that in many cases a person who became ill with a dangerous disease, and then recovered from it, never seemed to get the disease again. Pasteur's idea was to give young Joseph Meister a "small" case of rabies in the hope that this would somehow protect him from developing a full-blown, fatal case from the dog bites. Fortunately, the rabies-bitten boy lived, proving that Pasteur's inoculation technique could prevent a fatal rabies infection from occurring even after known contact with the disease had occurred.

Today, of course, we know why Pasteur's rabies vaccination worked. When an infectious organism invades a person's body, an army of antibodies is manufactured to help destroy the invader, thus allowing the body to

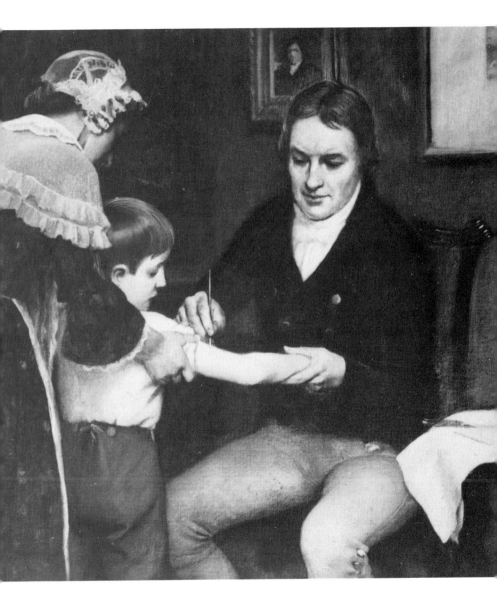

This painting of Edward Jenner in 1796 shows him performing his first vaccination on the boy James Phipps to protect him against smallpox.

recover. Some of that antibody army then remains in the bloodstream, and other parts of the immune system *remember the antigen* and stand ready to pounce as soon as the same invader turns up again. When a person is vaccinated against a particular disease, a small amount of harmless protein material from the infectious organism—the organism's identifying antigen—is introduced into the body to create a mock kind of infection. This can't actually make the person sick, but the body's immune system doesn't know that, and reacts exactly as if the infection were real. Antibodies are manufactured and rush to the area of the invasion. Phagocytes arrive on the scene, ready to do battle with the invader. The lymphocyte patrols swing into action, confirming that an invasion has taken place—as far as they can tell. Presently, things quiet down, after the antigen from the vaccine has been neutralized, but the immune system remains in a state of permanent alert against that antigen. And when the *real* invader comes along, even years later, the immune system immediately destroys it before it can even begin to cause an infection.

The exact material contained in a vaccine will vary from disease to disease. The vaccine against rubeola, for example, is made up of real, live measles viruses that have been weakened, or attenuated, in the laboratory so that they cannot cause a full-blown case of measles. Typhoid fever vaccine contains killed typhoid fever bacilli. The surface antigen from the dead shells of these bacteria alone can cause such a powerful immune system response in the body that the inoculation site often becomes sore and swollen for a day or so after the shot. Tetanus vaccine is not made from the bacteria at all, but from the extremely poisonous nerve toxin poured out by the tetanus organisms—the poison that causes the "lockjaw" symptoms of the disease. In the laboratory, this toxin is changed to a harmless form by treatment with formalin to produce a *toxoid* (a toxin like material that lacks the toxin's poisonous qualities). Vaccination with the tetanus toxoid alone triggers antibodies that prevent the dangerous effects of tetanus infection. The immune response to tetanus toxoid is so vigorous that high levels of antitoxin antibodies remain in the circulation for twenty years or more.

Today, in addition to those mentioned, we have highly effective vaccines to prevent diphtheria, pertussis (whooping cough), rubella (German measles), and polio, to name just a few. Travelers to foreign lands can be vaccinated against yellow fever, bubonic plague and cholera. One of the most recent vaccines to be developed can protect people from a dangerous viral infection of the liver known as hepatitis B. Indeed, in many ways immunization techniques have changed the whole world for the better. Polio vaccine, for example, had reduced the number of cases of paralytic polio from forty thousand a year in the late 1930s to a mere handful a year today. Pertussis (whooping cough) vaccine saves the lives of tens of thousands of babies annually. Smallpox vaccination, used worldwide, was the key to eliminating this terrible disease completely by 1974. In 1988 researchers are very close to perfecting a vaccine to prevent malaria, a disease that kills four million people every year worldwide, and immunologists around the world are facing a supreme challenge: finding a safe, effective vaccine to protect people from infection by the human immunodeficiency virus or HIV—which causes AIDS.

Certainly the immune system is swift and effective in protecting the body from foreign antigens. But sometimes it is a little too effective. It goes to work swiftly anytime it interprets anything in the body as a "not-self" antigen, whether that interpretation is correct or not. We might compare the immune system to an extremely high-strung and ill-tempered farmer standing out in his field with a loaded shotgun, ready to shoot the moment a suspicious-looking stranger is seen climbing over the fence. Of course the farmer might protect his farm very effectively this way, but if he happens to be a little *too* high-strung and ill-tempered, he might end up shooting out some of his own windows or even his own cow at the same time. And strange as it may seem, this is actually very much what the immune system does, on occasion, when it overreacts to a foreign invader, or turns on the body's own normal, healthy cells—by mistake!

5

THE IMMUNE SYSTEM AS VILLAIN

Ordinarily the immune system plays its role as protective hero quietly and efficiently, rarely calling attention to itself. Without it our lives would be a constant and ultimately losing battle against infections of all sorts. But there are several ways the immune system may also, on occasion, do harm to the body—sometimes very serious harm—taking on the role of villain rather than hero. One of the most frequent ways this happens is when the immune system works so well and reacts so vigorously to a foreign invader that the reaction itself can cause distressing symptoms. This can result in the *allergic reactions* we mentioned earlier.

TROUBLE WITH ALLERGIES

The immune system has no way to know which foreign invader may be deadly dangerous to the body and which may actually be perfectly harmless. Whatever the "not-self" substance may be, whether a deadly polio virus or such relatively innocent invaders as pollen grains, food proteins, or animal danders, the immune system springs into action and clears them away. What is more, after the first contact with such substances, the immune system remains alert, or sensitized, to any sign of re-invasion.

This is perfectly normal. But some people, because of their heredity, have immune systems that become *abnormally* sensitive to certain of these seemingly harmless substances. In these people, when the invading substance comes along a second time, the immune system seems to react more vigorously than normal. These people make enormous amounts of a class of antibodies called IgE antibodies, in response to very small doses of offending antigens. These IgE antibodies bind to and "arm" a group of large cells known as *mast cells* which are strategically located on body surfaces (the lining of the nose, for example, or the lining of the bronchi, or the skin or the intestinal lining). Reappearance of an offending antigen causes this overload of IgE to activate these armed mast cells, which then release chemicals which cause the symptoms we call "allergic." Large numbers of other special, allergy-related phagocytes called *eosinophiles* come piling in. Fluid begins pouring out of the cells, so that localized areas of swelling occur. Worst of all, a chemical substance known as *histamine*, normally present inside mast cells all over the body, is released into the fluid spaces between the cells. Histamine causes no problem at all when it is inside the cells, where it belongs, but outside the cells it acts like a fierce chemical irritant that causes tiny blood vessels to dilate, the blood pressure to fall, an outpouring of fluid into the tissue, and intense itching. (See figure 4.)

This kind of immune overreaction is based on an abnormal overproduction of IgE antibodies, and is rather like calling out the entire Coast Guard in order to repel

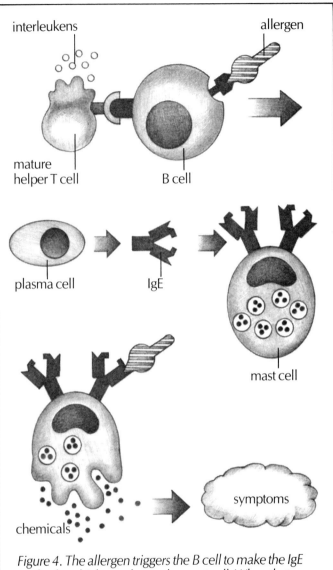

interleukens

allergen

mature
helper T cell

B cell

plasma cell

IgE

mast cell

chemicals

symptoms

Figure 4. The allergen triggers the B cell to make the IgE antibody, which attaches to the mast cell. When that allergen reappears, it binds to the IgE and triggers the mast cell to release its chemicals.

one small foreign fishing boat. The end result is what is called an allergic reaction. Allergic reactions demonstrate the enormous power the immune system can unleash if it is not properly regulated. Fortunately, for most of us, it is kept under tight regulation. But when an allergic reaction occurs, the exact form it may take depends in part on what area is exposed to the foreign antigen. When a pollen is at fault, for instance, the reaction is likely to center in the membranes of the eyes, nose, and upper respiratory tract, where pollen grains are drawn in and contact the moist, warm tissue. These membranes become swollen and red and begin pouring out a watery fluid. The histamine released into the tissues may cause violent sneezing and itching. As we saw in chapter one, this reaction is commonly called "hay fever," probably because ragweed, which flowers during the summer haying season, is one of the most commonly offending pollens.

Allergic reactions to food, insect bites, or medicines may produce a different problem—a characteristic skin reaction known as *urticaria*, or "hives." Large areas of the skin suddenly become red, swollen, puffy, and extremely itchy. Hives can appear while you watch them, become giant in size, and then melt into each other across the skin surface until the victim appears red and mottled all over. Then, just as suddenly and dramatically as they appear, they go away.

Another kind of allergic skin reaction, however, takes days or weeks to develop and tends to hang on much longer. This is *allergic eczema*. Eczema most commonly attacks infants or children, and may be related to an allergic reaction to certain food proteins. Patches of skin behind the knees, around the mouth, in the groin, or inside the elbows, become thickened, leathery, red-

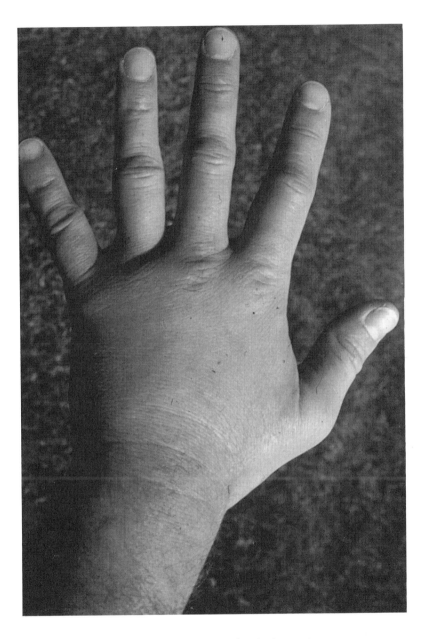

Swollen hand from multiple bee stings

dened, and extremely itchy. Presently the skin breaks down and begins oozing a sticky serum that dries and crusts on the surface. Bacterial infection, introduced by uncontrollable scratching, commonly complicates the picture. Medical treatment may only partly relieve the symptoms, but fortunately, many children seem to improve spontaneously as they grow older.

Asthma is sometimes caused by an allergic reaction to an inhaled antigen. This wheezing respiratory disorder can usually be controlled with medicines, but may recur in a chronic pattern for years in spite of treatment.

Of all the different forms of allergic reaction, however, perhaps the most frightening and dangerous is the reaction that can occur from exposure to drugs such as penicillin, or even as a result of bee stings. This rapid reaction, known as *anaphylactic shock*, can begin within minutes of contact with the offending allergen. The victim begins to wheeze. Giant hives may appear. The eyelids grow puffy, and the membranes inside the larynx (voice box) swell up, tending to choke off the main airway. At the same time, the blood pressure suddenly drops, and the person may faint or pass out because not enough blood is getting to the brain.

This shocklike reaction is quite rare, but can be very dangerous unless treated at once. Speedy treatment with hormones such as adrenalin and cortisone, together with antihistamine drugs, can reverse the reaction almost as quickly as it comes on. But once a person has had an anaphylactic reaction, he or she must take great pains to avoid another contact with the offending substance. This is not too hard with a medicine such as penicillin, but bee stings can be highly unpredictable. Today people who have had such a reaction from bee stings should carry emergency medicine with them, and consider being desensitized—that is, rendered less sensitive—to bee venom by means of a series of allergy shots, as protection against an unexpected violent reaction later.

Indeed, desensitization can sometimes be helpful in avoiding other kinds of allergic reactions as well. The person is given a series of injections containing tiny but increasingly large doses of the offending allergen (that is, the allergy-causing antigen) over a period of time. Gradually the body develops a tolerance to the substance, so that more and more is required to trigger an allergic reaction. In addition, the shots often stimulate the body to form *blocking antibodies*, which tend to diminish the vigor of the immune reaction, like a candle snuffer over a candle flame. Desensitization works better in some cases than others. It's a help to many people, but not a perfect answer to allergy problems. For the short term, many allergies can be prevented best simply by learning from experience what substances to avoid and then avoiding them, or using medications to suppress the symptoms when avoiding the substance is not possible.

HOST-VERSUS-GRAFT REACTIONS
AND IMMUNOSUPPRESSION

In recent years doctors treating very sick people have run headlong into another kind of difficult problem with the immune system: It stubbornly insists on rejecting and destroying foreign substances in the body even when the doctors, for very good reasons, don't want it to.

Since the 1940s and 1950s, doctors have found ways to prolong life by performing *organ transplants*—surgically removing diseased organs such as hearts or kidneys from dying patients and replacing them with healthy organs transplanted from voluntary donors, or from people who have died prematurely from auto accidents or other grave injuries. Surgeons can now perform such operations very successfully, and the transplanted organs function perfectly well, at first. Yet many such attempts either end in failure or are seriously hindered because the immune system swings vigorously into action to reject or throw off the "not-self" organ that has been transplanted.

Of course, we can't blame the immune system for doing this. After all, eliminating "not-self" is its prime directive, developed over millions of years of biological evolution, and it is merely doing what it is supposed to do, efficiently and effectively. Organ transplants are a modern biological invention of human beings. Nothing comparable has ever evolved anywhere in nature, so natural systems simply don't recognize this kind of human intervention as useful or natural. Indeed, the immune system doesn't recognize it *at all*. To a person whose very life depends on the function of a transplanted kidney or heart, being "protected" against the transplant by the immune system may be small comfort, but that is the way it is.

Thus the transplantation of virtually any organ or tissue from one person to another will be blocked by the immune system to some degree in what is called a host-versus-graft reaction or rejection reaction, unless something is done to prevent it. Such transplants, today called *allografts*, were once known as *homografts* from the Latin word *homo* meaning "same," because the grafted tissue or organ is taken from an individual of the same species. When tissue is taken from one part of a person's body and grafted onto another part of the same person—an *autograft*, or "same person" graft—there is no problem with rejection because the immune system recognizes the grafted tissue as "self" and therefore "okay." Similarly, transplanting an organ from one identical twin to the other will often work well because identical twins originally developed from the same fertilized egg cell and their cells contain the same basic genetic material. In such a case the immune system of one identical twin simply identifies protein material from the other one as "self."

Fortunately, immunologists have found some clever ways to fool the immune system—or at least suppress its activity—when an allograft organ transplant is necessary. The first step is to try to find an organ donor whose cells' proteins are as similar as possible to the "self" proteins of the person to receive the transplant. If the patient doesn't happen to have an identical twin handy, sometimes a brother, a sister, the mother, or the father may have similar enough proteins that the patient's immune system will be able to accept the transplanted organ as "self." Immunologists now have methods for "tissue-typing" to help determine the closeness or similarity between donor and recipient proteins.

Too often, however, even the closest possible match isn't close enough, and a dangerous rejection reaction occurs after a transplant has been grafted in place. When this happens, the recipient's immune system must somehow be artificially suppressed or crippled—put temporarily out of commission—so that the "not-self" organ can grow into place and function in peace. Powerful medicines can be given, for example, to prevent the swift growth of lymphocytes and antibody-producing plasma cells in the lymph nodes and bone marrow. At the same time, cortisonelike hormones can be given to suppress other aspects of the immune reaction. In the early 1980s an extremely powerful drug called *cyclosporine* was found to be very useful for suppressing an organ recipient's immune activity without many of the bad side effects of prolonged cortisone treatment. Thanks to such advances in immunosuppressive treatment, patients with heart transplants, for instance, have a far better chance of prolonged survival than before. But as soon as the treatment is stopped and the immune system recovers from suppression, it may begin once again to identify "not-self" proteins and swing into action to reject the transplant. Thus, in most such patients, immunosuppressive treatment must be repeated time and again, or continued indefinitely.

Unfortunately, immunosuppression itself can be very dangerous. When a person's immune system has been deliberately suppressed, it may stop rejecting a transplant organ, but it also stops fighting off dangerous infections. These patients must depend very heavily on antibiotic treatment to control bacterial infections and must constantly be on guard against viral infections. This dilemma is one of the reasons that progress in the use of organ transplants has been so painfully slow. Even today, only kidney transplants are really uniformly successful. One major goal of research in immunology today is to find better and safer ways to suppress the immune system so that organ transplants can be done more often and more safely.

IMMUNITY GONE WILD: AUTOIMMUNE DISEASES

Of all the ways the immune system can cause trouble, however, perhaps the most serious is when it starts mistaking normal "self" tissue in the body for "not-self" and begins attacking normal, healthy organs and tissues as if they were an enemy invader. This is essentially what happens in a number of serious disorders that doctors speak of as *autoimmune,* or "self-immune" diseases.

Nobody knows for sure exactly why the immune system sometimes behaves in this apparently wrong-headed way. We do know that the immune system is very efficient once it has been triggered into activity. And it is clear that something as yet unknown can sometimes happen to change the surface proteins on our own cells in such a way that the immune system, just doing its normal job, begins to interpret them as "not-self" and begins to attack them. Possibly, in some people, the immune system itself begins to break down in subtle ways and starts making terrible mistakes determining what is "self" and what is "not-self." In other people, malfunctioning or incorrect genes may trigger these changes; or the changes may be triggered by viruses. All we really know is that when the immune system begins attacking apparently normal, healthy cells and tissues, the result can be the appearance of certain long-term, destructive, or disabling diseases.

The most common of these is rheumatoid arthritis, a joint disease that attacks millions of people, women far more often than men. In some people, at some time between early childhood and middle age, the immune system begins attacking tissues around the finger joints, knees, spine, and other joints. Huge numbers of lymphocytes appear in these joint tissues. Pain, swelling, and redness develop. Fluid fills the joint spaces, and presently a steady destruction of the joint cartilage begins. Although the disease may get better or worse from time to time, and although many medicines are helpful in relieving the symptoms, there is so far no known cure for rheumatoid arthritis once it has started, and no way, in the long run, to prevent the crippling joint damage that slowly results in many victims.

Sometimes, when an autoimmune attack begins, it happens without warning, and almost unbelievably quickly. Recently, for example, researchers have found very strong evidence that so-called "juvenile" or Type 1 early-onset diabetes can be an autoimmune manifestation. Possibly some kind of virus infection first stimulates the immune system to make antibodies against the Beta-cells in the pancreas—the cells that normally manufacture *insulin*, the hormone our cells need to utilize sugars and other carbohydrate foods. The anti-Beta-cell antibodies then begin destroying these vital insulin-making cells. This type of diabetes usually appears very suddenly during childhood or the teen years, and is marked by a sudden severe shortage of insulin. Most Type I diabetics are permanently *insulin-dependent*— they have to take insulin by injection all their lives because their bodies just aren't making any. What is astonishing is how *swiftly* this autoimmune destruction of Beta-cells takes place. There is evidence that once the attack begins, virtually all the insulin-making Beta-cells in the pancreas may be wiped out in only twenty-four hours!

Until now, Type I diabetes has always been known as a lifelong, destructive disease. But the discovery that it is probably autoimmune in origin has raised hopes that it might be cured by administering immunosuppressive drugs, such as cyclosporine, at exactly the right time. And indeed, some early tests of such treatment are promising. If the drug is started soon enough after onset, the amount of insulin some patients need is reduced. This suggests that immunosuppression may save some

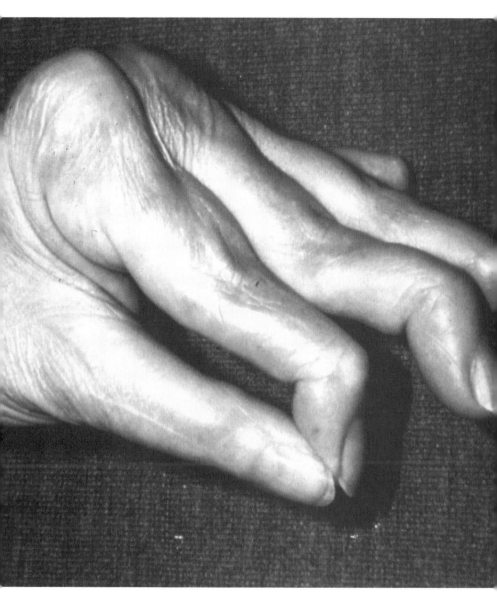

*This hand is crippled by rheumatoid arthritis,
the most common of the autoimmune diseases.*

*Multiple sclerosis (MS) is believed to
be an autoimmune disease that damages
the nerves and impairs their function.*

insulin-making cells from the immune system onslaught, or even allow them to recover.

Several other diseases are now also believed to be autoimmune. In one disabling condition known as lupus erythematosus, the immune system begins damaging tissues in the skin, blood vessels, heart, and kidneys. In multiple sclerosis (MS) the nerves are damaged and their function impaired, while in myasthenia gravis the muscle function is affected by an autoimmune reaction. All these diseases are still considered incurable, but huge sums of money are now being spent trying to learn about them. Some immunologists think there may be simple reasons for the immune system to turn against the body in certain cases, so that prevention or cure of these diseases may one day be possible. Other immunologists are not so optimistic—but only time and further research will tell.

6

THE IMMUNE SYSTEM DESTROYED

The immune system is an organ system like any other in the body, and it has its own vital job to do: protecting us from foreign invaders that can destroy us. As we have seen, it's an extremely complicated organ system, but the protection it provides is very real. With it, we can live long, healthy lives. Without it, we die.

Until recently the immune system itself rarely fell victim to disease or damage. A few people were born with defective immune systems, which gave them trouble. Certain cancers of the blood or lymph nodes—the leukemias or lymphomas—could cause serious damage to the immune system and lead to death. A few uncommon blood protein disorders could interfere with the immune system's function. But by and large, this organ system was the most remarkably trouble-free of any in the body.

Then, in the early 1980s, all this changed. A terrible immune-system destroyer appeared on the scene: a virus known as HIV—the *human immunodeficiency virus*—capable of infecting the human body and leading to a serious disease known as AIDS. Nothing that has ever happened before has made us realize more clearly how important the immune system is, or how devastating its destruction can be.

Of course, everyone has heard of AIDS, but many people don't understand clearly what causes it, or what it actually does to the body that is so bad. In brief, AIDS (short for *acquired immune deficiency syndrome*) is the most serious form of an infectious disease caused by a virus that probably first appeared in the United States sometime in the 1960s and began spreading rapidly in the early 1980s. The infection is spread from person to person by intimate sexual contact, by using needles or other drug-injecting equipment contaminated by infected blood, by receiving transfusions of HIV-infected blood, or by passing the deadly virus from infected mother to unborn baby through the placenta during pregnancy. And HIV infection can be deadly. In spite of new drugs that can help slow the progress of the disease, there is no cure, as yet, for HIV infection, nor any protective vaccine against it. Persons infected with the HIV virus who develop symptoms of the full-blown disease may die within a few months or years. The only other virus disease we know with such a record of fatality once symptoms of infections have appeared is rabies.*

THE DEADLY ATTACK

What is it about the HIV virus that makes it so deadly? We certainly know of some dreadful virus infections. Smallpox killed 30 to 40 percent of its victims during epidemics in Europe, and as many as 95 percent of some American Indian tribes that came into contact with it.

* For more detailed information about AIDS, see Nourse, Alan E., M.D.: *AIDS* (Revised Edition). New York: Franklin Watts, 1989.

Measles was probably a deadly virus in ancient Greece. Many victims of encephalitis (brain fever) viruses die, and some lesser-known viruses (the Lassa fever virus, or the Marburg virus, for example) have taken high tolls. But the body has had some defenses against these infections, because the immune system managed to fight them down, at least in some cases. So what is so different about HIV?

The answer is that the major organ system the HIV virus attacks is *the immune system itself.*

We all live in vulnerable human bodies with healthy immune systems to protect us from foreign invaders, including deadly viruses. Now let's try to imagine the most dangerous virus we can think of, the most deadly and destructive imaginable—what would it be like?

First of all, it would be a virus that would *directly destroy our major defense against viruses*—the immune system itself. It would attack the immune system by preference and just wipe it out—not the heart, not the lungs, not the liver, but *the immune system.*

What is more, it would not only hit the immune system, it would hit hardest at the very foundation stones of the immune system—the T-cells that make the whole system go. To make things worse, it would also hit the brain cells that make the whole *body* go, and would perhaps even use immune-system cells to carry the virus to the brain cells it would have trouble reaching otherwise. And finally, it would be transmitted from one person to another through one of the most common of all human activities—intimate sexual contact.

The virus we are describing would be living horror. And the virus we are describing is the HIV virus.

We know that the HIV virus, on entry into the body, at some point begins invading T-helper cells—the major triggering mechanism and control center of the whole

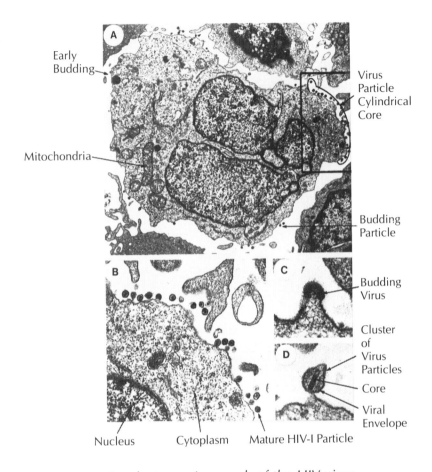

Early Budding

Virus Particle Cylindrical Core

Mitochondria

Budding Particle

Budding Virus

Cluster of Virus Particles

Core

Viral Envelope

Nucleus   Cytoplasm   Mature HIV-I Particle

An electron micrograph of the HIV virus attacking a white blood cell

immune system—and killing them. Without them, the B-cells cannot be helped to do their job correctly, and the plasma cells antibody factories can't make the appropriate, effective antibodies to fight off the new infection. The phagocytes don't get the message to go fight invaders; in fact, recent research suggests that one group of phagocytes, the macrophages, may become *carriers* of the HIV virus, transporting it to the brain, which it otherwise might not reach.

With fewer and fewer T-cells left, the immune system cannot fight off the HIV virus or any other foreign invader. In time, the entire immune system is destroyed. And then come the waves of infection—wave after wave—that the immune system would otherwise have fought off. Cancers appear that the immune system would otherwise have blocked and destroyed. Eventually many HIV-infected people fall victim to and die from overwhelming infection or uncontrollable cancer, the condition known as AIDS.

THE BATTLE AGAINST AIDS

There is no doubt that the battle against the HIV virus is going to be one of the most hard-fought and crucial battles in the whole history of medicine. Never have the stakes been so high—even the Black Plague epidemics in the Middle Ages killed only 25 percent of their victims. Never before has a single disease threatened our lives so intimately.

What can be done about it? One obvious thing might be to find ways to strengthen and rebuild the AIDS patient's crippled immune system. The trouble is, we *don't know how to get around the invading HIV virus.* It's as simple as that. In every attempt to restore the immune system, HIV simply infects and destroys it again. We have learned more about the immune system in the few years since AIDS first struck than in all the previous two hundred years put together, but there is no way yet known to destroy HIV so the immune system can be restored.

What about attacking the virus directly with antiviral drugs and antibiotics? Unfortunately, most viruses aren't affected much by drugs or antibiotics, and HIV is no exception. True, there are drugs like *zudovidine* (better known as "AZT") that seem to interfere with the virus's activity in the body, to some degree. It can prolong life and reduce the symptoms of AIDS, so the victims can lead more normal, comfortable lives—but there are no *curative* drugs on the horizon. So what about making a vaccine to prevent the infection? Once again, we just don't know how to make an effective vaccine against HIV. Much research is concentrated on this problem, and probably such a vaccine finally will be found for widespread use—but this might not be for years.

Meanwhile, the one thing we *do* know how to do is protect ourselves from infection: by adhering to safe sex practices, by avoiding possibly contaminated drug-injection equipment, by testing all transfusion blood against contamination, and by judicious use of voluntary testing for HIV to prevent spread of the infection to others, including unborn babies.*

If there is one *good* thing the AIDS epidemic had done, it has been to focus researchers' attention on the importance of the immune system, and to force us to study this vital organ system more intensively than we ever would have studied it otherwise. And this widespread study may lead to far more than just ways to prevent, control, or cure AIDS.

* For more information about protecting yourself from AIDS and other sexually transmitted diseases, see Nourse, Alan E., *AIDS* (Revised Edition), New York, Franklin Watts, 1989; and *Teen Guide to Safe Sex*, New York, Franklin Watts, 1988.

7

SOME FRONTIERS OF IMMUNITY

For obvious reasons, immunology—the study of the immune system—is one of the busiest of all areas of medical research today. The more scientists learn about the immune system, the more they realize how deeply it is involved in many everyday aspects of health and disease. It can do immeasurable good for the body on the one hand, and serious harm on the other. And like all other organ systems, it is vulnerable to irreparable damage. Researchers today are studying it from all three standpoints.

They are searching for ways to enhance its natural protective function—to capitalize on the good things it can do to protect us against many dangerous diseases and invaders. They are also hoping to find better ways to control the immune system in order to deal more effectively with allergies, rejection reactions, and autoimmune diseases. And—most pressingly, in light of AIDS—they are searching for ways to prevent or treat infections that affect the immune system itself.

In this widespread study, one of the most important areas of investigation, maybe even more important than AIDS, is the search for a better understanding of the connection between the immune system and the body's fight against cancer.

IMMUNOLOGY AND CANCER

Nobody knows precisely why cancer starts. Something happens in the body that causes certain cells to change into something slightly different and abnormal. Among other things, these abnormal or altered cells begin to grow and divide far more swiftly than is normal. A single wildly growing cell soon becomes a cluster of sick cells, and then a lump, or tumor. Presently these abnormal cells begin to invade surrounding tissues, crowding out normal cells, and a full-blown cancer develops. At some point, cancer cells become unglued from the original tumor and travel to distant parts of the body, where they lodge and grow into new tumors. In some cases viruses are known to play a part in changing normal cells into cancer cells. In other cases pollutants in the environment, chemicals in tobacco smoke, or substances in the foods we eat may lead directly or indirectly to cancerous changes in cells.

Modern research has shown that the immune system is deeply involved in fighting cancer when it first begins. It is now believed that when a normal cell changes into a cancer cell, the immune system somehow learns that a change has occurred and tries to do something about it. Even though the cell was originally "self" and therefore "okay," when it becomes cancerous certain subtle changes may occur in its surface proteins. The immune system detects a change from "self" to "not quite self" and sets out to destroy the altered cell before it can become an actively growing cancer, even though cancers produce very few specific "not-self" antigens.

In fact, there is evidence suggesting that in most cases the immune system wins the battle. Many cancer experts are convinced that a certain number of previously normal cells in the body are becoming cancer cells all the time, probably from childhood on, with the immune system searching out and destroying each one as it becomes abnormal. According to this view, it is only when the immune system misses one of these dangerously altered cells, or when a group of changed cells "break away" from immune-system control, that cancer as we know it has a chance to begin developing.

Even then, immunologists believe, the immune system continues the fight. It may destroy the cancerous growth at the two-cell, four-cell, or eight-cell stage of development—and may even carry on the fight as the tumor grows larger. In some forms of cancer special cells—killer lymphocytes, the "natural killer cells" or NK cells we spoke of earlier, or T-cells with special cell-destroying capabilities—are known to cluster around the cancerous growth, knocking out as many of the cancerous cells as possible. In other cases, special substances produced in collaboration with the immune system seem to slow down the growth of cancer cells.

One such group of substances, discovered in 1957, are special proteins known as *interferons* because they seem to interfere in some way with the spread of viral infections or the growth of cancer cells. Several groups of interferons are now known, some of them produced by the cells that form fibrous tissues, and some by other tissue cells in the body. Early testing with advanced cancer patients has shown that large doses of certain interferons seem to slow down the growth of the cancer, at least temporarily. But natural interferons are made only in very tiny amounts in the body. It was only when scientists learned how to produce large quantities of interferons in the laboratory by means of *genetic-engineering techniques* (see p. 84) that large doses of these substances became available. And unfortunately, large doses can be very toxic to the patient. So far, we know that interferons are effective in treating some kinds of leukemia and a cancer known as Kaposi's sarcoma, which often occurs in people with AIDS. Only further study will show how useful this kind of cancer *immunotherapy* may be with other cancers.

Another form of experimental immunotherapy against cancer involves the use of strange substances known as *monoclonal antibodies*. Immunologists have recently learned how to make a weird new type of laboratory cell by getting cancer cells from a mouse to join or merge with human lymphocytes to form a cluster of "hybrid" cells known as a *hybridoma* in the laboratory. When made with the right human lymphocytes, these hybridoma cells can then produce special antibodies that are drawn directly to cancer cells. When molecules of anticancer drugs are hooked onto these monoclonal antibodies, the drug is then, in theory, drawn directly to the cancer along with the antibody and can destroy the cancer cells without hurting normal cells around it. Many problems must be solved before these "magic bullets" can be used widely against cancer in humans; they simply illustrate one more way that frontier research in immunology is involved in the fight against cancer.

NEW VACCINES FOR
OLD DISEASES

On another frontier of immunology, scientists are continuing the search started almost two hundred years ago by Edward Jenner to find vaccines to protect us against dangerous infections, especially some that are still very difficult to treat effectively.

Consider malaria, for example. This terrible disease of recurring chills and fever is caused by a tiny one-celled animal parasite transmitted to millions of new victims every year by the bite of infected *Anopheles* mosquitoes. Even though malarial parasites are very definitely "not-self" invaders, the immune system has never been very good at destroying these organisms once they are entrenched in the body. The parasite buries itself in red blood cells to begin with, and then takes on several different forms in its life cycle. Further, its surface markers somehow are not clearly enough "not-self" for the immune system to detect them easily. For years various medicines have been used to fight malaria, but recently new drug-resistant strains of the parasite have appeared, so that more and more new malaria victims are getting a form of the disease that cannot readily be cured.

In this situation, immunologists have searched for a vaccine against the malaria parasite, something to stimulate the immune system in advance so that when the parasite gains entry into the body, the immune system can do a better job of eradicating it. And now, after years of failure, a safe, effective malaria vaccine is close at hand. As this is written, several promising "candidate vaccines" are actually being tested, and one in particular looks very good. Thanks to research in immunology, the days of malaria as a major killer may soon be over.

The search for a vaccine against hepatitis B, a dangerous viral infection of the liver, was also solved by dogged research. This disease, also known as serum hepatitis, is most commonly passed from person to person by way of sexual contact, contaminated hypodermic needles or drug-injecting equipment, or—in some cases—through transfusions of contaminated blood. Some 1 to 2 percent of all victims die, while another 5 to 10 percent develop long-lasting or chronic liver infection after the acute illness subsides. Still others seem to get well but remain carriers of the live virus for years, constantly capable of infecting others.

Immunologists had long been eager to develop a vaccine against this dangerous disease, especially to protect hospital workers or people who must have frequent blood transfusions, artificial kidney treatments, or frequent injections of medicines. But the search involved many special problems. The first task was to identify and isolate the hepatitis B virus itself. This alone took decades of work. Next, some protein marker or antigen related to the virus had to be found that could be injected as a vaccine, to stimulate the immune system into producing anti-hepatitis B antibodies. At last, just the right surface protein antigen was isolated from cultures of the virus, but in such very tiny quantities and at such great expense that it wasn't practical to try to use it as a vaccine.

At this point researchers called upon a brand-new laboratory technique known as *genetic engineering* to find a solution to the problem. In brief, genetic engineering involves the manipulation of the genetic or hereditary material in living cells—particularly the DNA molecules that form the genes and chromosomes—in order to make those cells produce protein materials they would not normally manufacture. In the case of hepatitis B surface antigen, scientists found ways to remove DNA molecules from the interior of certain simple and harmless bacteria, break those DNA molecules apart into chunks, and then "splice" (join) segments taken from different DNA molecules that carried the "manufacturing code" for the particular hepatitis B surface protein that was needed. By using this gene-splicing technique, the altered DNA could then be returned to the bacterial cells, and those cells would then begin producing the desired protein in large enough quantities to make a practical hepatitis B vaccine.

The technique worked. By "harvesting" the surface protein antigen from gene-spliced bacterial cultures, it was possible to mass-produce a vaccine that proved highly effective in preventing hepatitis B infections. The vaccine was finally approved by the U.S. Food and Drug Administration in November 1981 and is now widely used to protect people who are at high risk of contracting this disease, such as hospital and lab workers.

There is no question that immunologists in the future will be using more and more front-line research techniques such as genetic engineering to learn more about how the immune system works, how it can be controlled, and how it can be manipulated for the achievement of better health. For example, in recent years a lab technique known as *radioimmunoassay* has proven extremely useful for identifying and measuring the quantities of various protein substances in the body that previously were difficult or impossible to measure at all.

The science of immunology had its faltering beginnings almost two hundred years ago, as a few medical pioneers began to realize that the human body had a built-in protective mechanism to guard it against alien invaders of many kinds. But only in the last few decades have we begun to understand how very complex the immune system really is, how beautifully it works to protect us, how dangerous it can be in certain circumstances, and above all, how badly we need it. In the decades to come, further knowledge and understanding will enable us to use the immune system's natural protection more effectively—and, we hope, to find out how to rebuild it when it is damaged and how best to prevent or repair the damage it sometimes can inflict.

GLOSSARY

AIDS (acquired immune deficiency syndrome)—the severe, symptomatic form of an infection caused by the HIV virus that destroys the T-helper cells of the immune system.

Allergic reaction or *allergy*—an abnormal and often overvigorous immune reaction to an invading foreign substance or antigen.

Allograft—the transplant of an organ or tissue from one person's body into another's. Sometimes spoken of as a *homograft*.

Anaphylactic shock—a particularly sudden, severe and life-threatening body-wide allergic reaction.

Antibodies—special gamma globulin protein molecules manufactured in the body to help neutralize or destroy foreign substances or antigens that have gained entry into the body.

Antigen—any foreign substance, usually containing protein, that can stimulate the production of antibodies when it gets into the body. It is sometimes called an *immunogen* because it *generates* an *immune* response in the body.

Antihistamine—a medicine that blocks the effect of *histamine* released into the tissues during an allergic reaction, and thus helps relieve allergic symptoms.

Antitoxin—an antibody formed to neutralize a bacterial poison, or *toxin*, that has entered the body.

Autograft—the transplant of an organ or tissue from one part of a person's body to another location in that person's body.

Autoimmune diseases—diseases that arise, at least in part, when a body's immune defense system attacks the person's own normal tissue. An example is rheumatoid arthritis.

Bacteria—one-celled plantlike organisms that in some cases can cause infections.

B-cells—a type of *lymphocyte* (a white blood cell) which can mature into a *plasma cell* and manufacture antibodies to help fight infections.

Cancer—a group of diseases in which previously normal cells begin to divide and grow abnormally fast, forming tumors and invading and destroying surrounding normal tissue.

Cellular defense system—that part of our immune defense system made up of white blood cells—phagocytes and lymphocytes—that can work to attack and destroy invading organisms.

Chemotaxis—a sort of "chemical signaling" system by which phagocytes at a distance are "called" to the site of an infection.

Combined immunodeficiency disease—a rare condition in which a baby is born with no T or B lymphocytes. Multiple severe infections and early death are common.

Complement molecules—special proteins in the bloodstream that work with antibodies to destroy invading foreign substances.

Cyclosporin—a powerful drug that can suppress immune-system activity and thus help prevent rejection of organ transplants.

Gamma globulin—a family of protein molecules in which all antibodies are found.

Genetic engineering—A whole variety of modern laboratory techniques to manipulate hereditary materials in living cells (such as the DNA molecules that form the genes and chromosomes) in order to make those cells manufacture proteins they would not normally manufacture.

Histamine—a natural body substance released into the tissue by mast cells during an allergic reaction. Histamine in the tissues causes much of the itching, swelling, and discomfort of allergies.

Humoral defense system—that part of the immune defense system consisting of chemical substances (antibodies or complement molecules) dissolved in the bloodstream and capable of neutralizing or destroying foreign invaders.

Immunity—the condition of being protected against, or *immune to*, a specific infection because of stimulation of the body's immune defense system.

Immunization—the process of rendering a person immune to a disease by deliberately introducing harmless foreign substances into the body. An example is immunization of a person against poliomyelitis by administering polio vaccine containing live but weakened polio viruses.

Immunoglobulins or *Ig's*—various forms of antibodies. Common forms of Ig's include IgA, IgG, IgM, and IgE.

Immunology—the scientific study of the component parts of our immune defense system and how they work.

Immunosuppressants—various drugs or chemicals that can temporarily suppress or block the activity of the immune defense system so that it cannot, for example, cause the rejection of a
transplanted organ.

Immunotherapy—stimulating parts of the immune system to treat
disease. Examples are the use of interferons, products of the
immune system, to treat cancer; or the use of allergy injections
to suppress "hay fever."

Interferons—special protein substances manufactured in tiny quantities by white blood cells and other tissues to interfere with the
growth of invading viruses, cancer cells, and so on.

Lymph channels or *lymphatics*—a microscopic network of channels
carrying body fluids between the cells of the body. Lymphocytes
(a form of white blood cells) can move freely around the body
through these channels.

Lymph nodes—small lumps of tissue (often incorrectly called "lymph
glands") distributed along the lymph channels.

Lymphocytes—small, free-moving cells with large nuclei that are
manufactured in the bone marrow and make up one class of
white blood cells. Different kinds of lymphocytes, including
B-cells, T-cells, and natural killer cells or NK cells, play many
important roles in the body's immune defense system.

Macrophages—large amoebalike white blood cells that travel
through the body, engulfing and destroying invading bacteria.
They are one form of *phagocytes*, or "cells that eat."

Mast cells—special immune cells, found in the lining of the nose,
bronchial tubes, and intestine, which release histamine into the
tissues during allergic reactions.

Memory cells—mature B-cells that carry a permanent impression of
the surface markers or antigens of a foreign invader as a guard
against future attack.

Monoclonal antibodies—artificial antibodies that have been targeted
at specific foreign invaders—such as cancer cells—and can be
used to carry a lethal drug "package" directly to the targeted
cells.

Natural killer cells or *NK cells*—special lymphocytes that can directly
and spontaneously attack and kill foreign cells such as cancer
cells in the body.

Phagocytes—various forms of white blood cells capable of engulfing
and digesting invading bacteria.

Plasma cells—cells in the bone marrow or lymph nodes that manufacture antibodies and that are derived from B-lymphocytes or
B-cells.

Radioimmunoassay—a complex but inexpensive form of laboratory test that uses antibodies to identify many different kinds of protein in the body.

Surface-marker molecules—molecules on the surface of cells that identify, or "mark," the kind of cells they are. Traveling lymphocytes react with these surface markers to determine whether a given cell is "self" or "not-self."

T-cells—lymphocytes influenced by the *thymus gland* during their development. T-cells act as the major controllers and regulators of the immune protective system. Among other kinds of T-cells, there are *T-helper cells* that speed up the production of antibodies by the plasma cells; and *T-suppressor cells* that slow down or suppress that activity when an alien invasion is defeated.

Toxin—a deadly kind of chemical poison sometimes produced by invading bacteria.

Toxoid—a toxin that has been deactivated until it is harmless, but can be used as a vaccine against the bacteria that produces the original toxin.

Vaccination—inoculation of a person with a modified virus, bacterial protein, or other substance to stimulate an immune response.

Vaccine—any serum or preparation containing an antigen that will stimulate an immune response.

Viruses—tiny microorganisms that are always much smaller than bacteria and are composed of DNA or RNA within a protein envelope. Viruses can invade body cells and cause viral infections.

ADDITIONAL READING

Dunlop, Marilyn. *Body Defenses: The Marvels and Mysteries of the Immune System*. New York: Avon, 1986.

Golos, Natalie, and Golbita, Francis G. *Coping with Your Allergies*. New York: Simon & Schuster, 1986.

Gutnik, Martin. *Immunology: From Pasteur to the Search for an AIDS Vaccine*. New York: Franklin Watts, 1989.

Leinwand, Gerald. *Transplants: Today's Medical Miracles*. New York: Franklin Watts, 1985.

Metos, Thomas. *Communicable Diseases*. New York: Franklin Watts, 1987.

Potts, Eva, and Morra, Marion. *Understanding Your Immune System*. New York: Longman, 1988.

INDEX

B-cells (continued)
   reproduction, 41
   and T-helper cells, 75–76
   transformation of, 38, 42
Bee stings, 16, 50, 61, 62–63
Behring, Emil von, 21
Black Plague, 77
B-lymphocytes. See B-cells
Body fluids, 25, 33, 37, 40,
   58, 67
Bone marrow, 12, 29, 31, 33
Breast milk, 25, 26
Bubonic plague, 55

Cancer, 44, 73, 77, 80–82, 88
Cellular defense system, 23, 88
Chemotaxis, 37, 88
Cholera, 55
Colds, 48
Complement molecules, 39–
   41, 43, 88
Cyclosporine, 66, 68, 88

Diabetes, 68, 70
Diphtheria, 21, 23, 48, 55
DNA, 84–85

Eczema, 60–62
Eosinophiles, 58

Fungi, 19

Gamma globulin, 25, 88
Genetic engineering, 82, 84–
   85, 88
Genetics, 27, 34, 51, 65, 84–
   85

Hay fever, 13–15, 60
Hepatitis B, 55, 83–85
Heredity. See Genetics
Histamine, 58, 60, 88
HIV (human immunodefi-
   ciency virus). See AIDS

Hives, 60, 62
Hormones, 62, 65, 68
Humoral defense system, 23,
   88
Hybridoma, 82

Immune system
   allergic reactions, 57–63
   antibodies, 21–24
   baby's, 26
   and cancer, 80–82
   control of, 79
   and HIV virus, 73–78
   immunization, 51–56
   immunoglobins, 25–27
   lack of, 10–13
   lymphocytes as foundation,
      30, 33
   natural immunity, 50
   NK cells as destroyers, 43–
      46
   and normal tissue, 66–71
   overactive, 13–17
   purpose, 9–10, 48–50,
      79–80
   reaction to infection, 36–
      41, 79–80
   reaction to second infec-
      tion, 41–42
   research on, 20–23, 79–
      80, 82–86
Immunity, 50, 89
Immunization and vaccination,
   42, 88, 90
   action of, 51–55
   for HIV infection, 74, 78
   current research, 82–85
   purpose, 51–52
   types of, 52–55
Immunodeficiency disease, 10–
   13, 73, 88
Immunoglobins (IGs), 25–27,
   51, 58, 88
Immunology, 8, 89

Immunosuppressants, 66, 68, 89
Immunosuppression, 63–66
Immunotherapy, 82, 89
Infections
    in AIDS, 77, 78
    antibodies and, 27, 39
    in babies, 26
    bacteria causing, 66
    in cancer, 81
    in diabetes, 68
    immune system effect, 41–42, 57, 79
    inhibition, 37
    virus causing, 31, 66, 83
Influenza, 19, 48
Inoculation. See Immunization and vaccination
Insulin, 68, 70
Interferons, 81–82, 89

Jenner, Edward, 52, 53, 83

Kaposi's sarcoma, 82

Leukemia, 73, 82
Local inflammatory reaction, 37
Lupus erythematosus, 71
Lymph channels, 33, 35, 37, 89
Lymph nodes, 89
    cancer of, 73
    lymphocytes in, 31, 33, 35–36
    plasma cells in, 29, 65
Lymphocytes, 89
    action of, 33, 35–36, 43–44
    in arthritis, 67
    in cancer, 81, 82
    formation, 31
    growth suppression, 65
    as immune system foundation, 30,33

plasma cell creation, 29
reaction to vaccination, 54
types, 33–34, 43

Macrophages, 43, 89
    function, 21, 22, 23
    as HIV virus carrier, 77
    lymphocyte interaction, 34, 36
Malaria, 55, 83
Mast cells, 58, 89
Measles, 48, 49, 50, 54, 55, 74
Memory cells, 38, 42, 43, 48, 89
Metchnikoff, Élie, 20–21, 23, 31
Microorganisms, 19–20
Mold spores, 15–16
Molecules. See Complement molecules; Surface-marker molecules
Monoclonal antibodies, 82, 89
Mucous membranes, 25, 36, 60, 62
Multiple sclerosis, 70, 71
Mumps, 48
Myasthenia gravis, 71

Natural killer cells (NK cells), 43–46, 81, 89
"Not-self" and "self" markers, 57
    in autoimmune diseases, 66–67
    in cancer, 80
    in malaria, 83
    in organ transplants, 64–65
    purpose, 34, 35, 37, 51
    in second infection, 42
    and T-cells, 37–38
    virus reaction, 44

S-4-11   LU6/06   4circs   13 libs